GREAT MINDS® WIT & WISDOM

# Grade K Module 3:
# America, Then and Now

## Student Edition

## COPYRIGHT STATEMENT

Published by Great Minds®.

Copyright ©2016 Great Minds®. All rights reserved. No part of this work may be reproduced or used in any form or by any means—graphic, electronic, or mechanical, including photocopying or information storage and retrieval systems—without written permission from the copyright holder.

ISBN: 978-1-68386-019-8

# Table of Contents

Handout 2A: Picture Hunt

Handout 8A: Home and School Sort

Handout 14A: Little House Cutout

Handout 17A: Question Cards

Handout 17B: Who, Does What Words

Handout 18A: Question Grab Bag Cards

Handout 19A: Communication and Transportation Sort

Handout 20A: End Punctuation Bingo

Handout 25A: Invention Cards

Handout 26A: Plural Words Cards

Handout 27A: End-of-Module Evidence Organizer

Handout 29A: Informative Poster Checklist

Volume of Reading Reflection Questions

*Wit & Wisdom* Parent Tip Sheet

# Name:

# Handout 2A: Picture Hunt

Directions: Circle the objects below that match with items in the illustrations of *When I Was Young in the Mountains.*

# Name:

# Handout 8A: Home and School Sort

**Directions:** Cut out the pictures at the bottom. Glue items from home in the Home column. Glue items from school in the School column.

| Home | School |
|---|---|
|  |  |

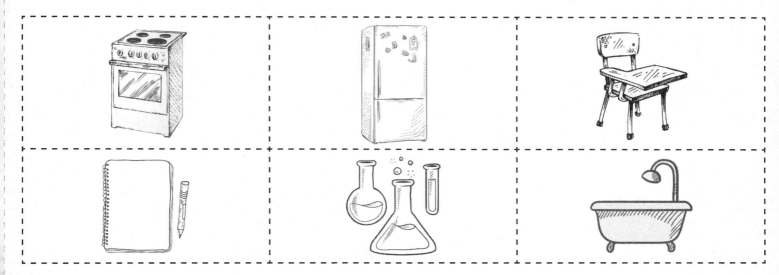

# Name:

# Handout 14A: Little House Cutout

**Directions:** Cut out the picture below. Fold as shown by the light-gray lines to create your own Little House.

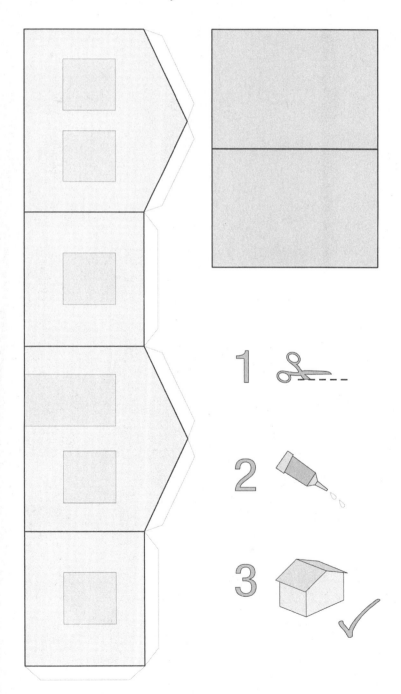

Name: _____

# Handout 17A: Question Cards

**Directions:** Use one card to ask a peer a question during a group discussion.

| **?** How did the Little House feel about the changes? | **?** How did the Little House feel about the changes? |
|---|---|
| **?** How did the Little House feel about the changes? | **?** How did the Little House feel about the changes? |
| **?** How did the Little House feel about the changes? | **?** How did the Little House feel about the changes? |
| **?** How did the Little House feel about the changes? | **?** How did the Little House feel about the changes? |

# Name:

# Handout 17B: Who, Does What Words

**Directions:** Write a person or thing example in each "Who" box. Write an action word example in each "Does What" box.

| 1. | Who: |
|----|------|
| 2. | Does What: |
| 3. | Who: |
| 4. | Does What: |
| 5. | Who: |

Name: _____

# Handout 18A: Question Grab Bag Cards

**Directions:** Cut out the cards and place them in the Grab Bag. Reach into the bag and pick one card. Use the selected question word to ask a question about the text.

| Who?  | What?  |
| --- | --- |
| Where? 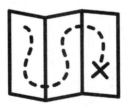 | When?  |
| Why?  | How? H |

# Name:

# Handout 19A: Communication and Transportation Sort

**Directions:** Cut out the pictures at the bottom. Glue communication items in the Communication column. Glue transportation items in the Transportation column.

| Communication | Transportation |
| --- | --- |
|  |  |

# Name:

# Handout 20A: End Punctuation Bingo

**Directions:** Listen to the sentence. Determine which punctuation mark goes at the end. Color one box with that mark.

| . | ? | ! |
|---|---|---|
| ? | . | ? |
| . | ! | . |

# Name:

# Handout 25A: Invention Cards

**Directions:** Cut out the cards and place them in a bag. Reach into the bag and pick one card. Use the selected invention for your Focusing Question Task.

| Bifocals | Long Arm |
|---|---|
|  |  |
| Flippers | Odometer |
|  |  |
| City Services | |
|    | |

# Name:

# Handout 26A: Plural Words Cards

**Directions:** Cut along the dotted line to form a set of cards. Use the illustrations to say a sentence using a plural word.

# Name:

# Handout 27A: End-of-Module Evidence Organizer

**Directions:** Draw and label the evidence you will use for your End-of-Module Task.

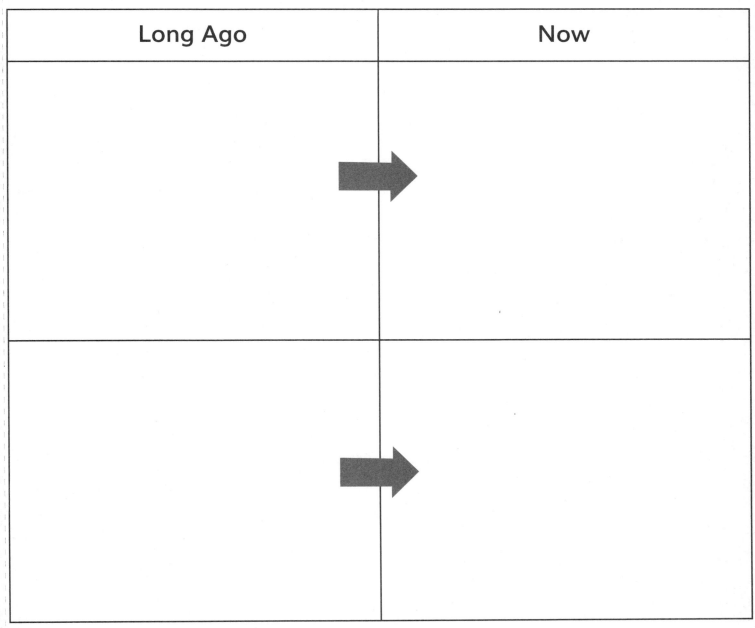

| Long Ago | Now |
|---|---|
|  |  |
|  |  |

Name: _____

# Handout 29A: Informative Poster Checklist

Directions: Circle ☺ yes or 😐 not yet to answer each question.

| Reading Comprehension | Self | Peer | Teacher |
|---|---|---|---|
| I chose information about "long ago" and "now" from the same detail in the text. | ☺ Yes   😐 Not Yet | ☺ Yes   😐 Not Yet | ☺ Yes   😐 Not Yet |
| **Structure** | **Self** | **Peer** | **Teacher** |
| I wrote a title for my poster. | ☺ Yes   😐 Not Yet | ☺ Yes   😐 Not Yet | ☺ Yes   😐 Not Yet |
| I wrote a topic statement. | ☺ Yes   😐 Not Yet | ☺ Yes   😐 Not Yet | ☺ Yes   😐 Not Yet |
| I wrote two details about my topic "long ago." | ☺ Yes   😐 Not Yet | ☺ Yes   😐 Not Yet | ☺ Yes   😐 Not Yet |
| I wrote two details about my topic "now." | ☺ Yes   😐 Not Yet | ☺ Yes   😐 Not Yet | ☺ Yes   😐 Not Yet |

# Name: _____

| Development | Self | | Peer | | Teacher | |
|---|---|---|---|---|---|---|
| I got my information from a module text. | ☺ Yes | 😐 Not Yet | ☺ Yes | 😐 Not Yet | ☺ Yes | 😐 Not Yet |
| **Style** | Self | | Peer | | Teacher | |
| I drew pictures to add information to my poster. | ☺ Yes | 😐 Not Yet | ☺ Yes | 😐 Not Yet | ☺ Yes | 😐 Not Yet |
| **Conventions** | Self | | Peer | | Teacher | |
| I wrote sentences that tell "who did what." | ☺ Yes | 😐 Not Yet | ☺ Yes | 😐 Not Yet | ☺ Yes | 😐 Not Yet |
| I spelled words using all the sounds I know. | ☺ Yes | 😐 Not Yet | ☺ Yes | 😐 Not Yet | ☺ Yes | 😐 Not Yet |

# Volume of Reading Reflection Questions

*America, Then and Now*, Kindergarten, Module 3

Student Name:

Text:

Author:

Topic:

Genre/type of book:

After reading your book, share what you know about how things were a long time ago and how things are now. Draw a picture or tell your teacher your answer to each question.

# Informational

1. **Wonder:** What do you notice about this book from its front and back cover? What questions do you have about this book?

2. **Organize:** What main ideas are discussed in this book? Point to the key details that you noticed.

3. **Reveal:** What do the illustrations in this book teach you about whether this book is "now" or "then?" Point to a picture in the book, and explain what you learned from looking closely.

4. **Distill:** What big idea did the author want you to learn about in this book? How does this big idea connect to another book you've read?

5. **Know:** What new information do you now know about life long ago? Share the new information that you learned.

6. **Vocabulary:** What are three words that you can use to describe one object in an illustration? Draw the object, and label it with the three describing words.

# Literary

1. **Wonder:** What are you noticing in this story?

2. **Organize:** What happened in this story? Quietly act out the story without saying a word or draw three pictures showing the beginning, middle, and end.

3. **Reveal:** Choose one illustration in the "long ago" story. How would that scene be different now?

4. **Distill:** Did any of the characters in this story learn a lesson? What lesson did they learn? Is it a lesson you could use in your life today?

5. **Know:** What have you learned about life long ago by reading this book?

6. **Vocabulary:** Find three new action words in the story. Act them out. How are they similar? How are they different?

# WIT & WISDOM PARENT TIP SHEET

## WHAT IS MY KINDERGARTEN STUDENT LEARNING IN MODULE 3?

Wit & Wisdom is our English curriculum. It builds knowledge of key topics in history, science, and literature through the study of excellent texts. By reading and responding to stories and nonfiction texts, we will build knowledge of the following topics:

Module 1: The Five Senses

Module 2: Once Upon a Farm

**Module 3: America, Then and Now**

Module 4: The Continents

In this third module, *America, Then and Now*, we will study how certain aspects of American life have changed over time. As we explore the past and the present, we ask the question: How has life in America changed over time?

## OUR CLASS WILL READ THESE BOOKS:

### Picture Books (Informational)

- *When I Was Young in the Mountains*, Cynthia Rylant
- *Home Then and Now*, Robin Nelson
- *School Then and Now*, Robin Nelson
- *Transportation Then and Now*, Robin Nelson
- *Communication Then and Now*, Robin Nelson
- *Now & Ben: The Modern Inventions of Benjamin Franklin*, Gene Baretta

### Picture Books (Literary)

- *The Little House*, Virginia Lee Burton

### Poem

- "Now We Are Six," A.A. Milne

## OUR CLASS WILL EXAMINE THIS PAINTING:

- *Washington Crossing the Delaware*, Emanuel Leutze

## OUR CLASS WILL LISTEN TO THESE SONGS:

- "Engine on the Track," *Gayle's Preschool Rainbow*
- "You're a Grand Old Flag," George M. Cohan
- "This Land Is Your Land," Woody Guthrie

## OUR CLASS WILL WATCH THIS VIDEO:

- "Sounds of a Glass Armonica," *Toronto Star*

## OUR CLASS WILL VIEW THIS WEBSITE:

- "Betsy Ross and the American Flag: Flag Picture Gallery," Independence Hall Association

## OUR CLASS WILL VIEW THESE PHOTOGRAPHS:

- *Old Hand Water Pump*, Judson McCranie
- Photographs from the article "Then & Now: The Stunning Speed of Urban Development," S.A. Rogers

## OUR CLASS WILL ASK THESE QUESTIONS:

- How was Cynthia Rylant's life different from your life?
- How has life at home and at school changed in America?
- What changes does the Little House see in her neighborhood?
- How have communication and transportation changed in America?
- How did Benjamin Franklin's inventions make life in America easier?

## QUESTIONS TO ASK AT HOME:

As you read with your Kindergarten student, ask

- What is the essential meaning of, or most important message in, this book?

## BOOKS TO READ AT HOME:

- *The White House*, Lisa M. Herrington
- *The American Flag*, Lisa M. Herrington
- *The Secret Subway*, Shana Corey
- *Mr. Ferris and His Wheel*, Kathryn Gibbs Davis
- *Maybelle the Cable Car*, Virginia Lee Burton
- *This Is New York*, Miroslav Sasek
- *This Is Washington, D.C.*, Miroslav Sasek
- *Brick by Brick*, Charles R. Smith, Jr.
- *I Have a Dream*, Martin Luther King, Jr. and Kadir Nelson
- *Here Come the Girl Scouts! The Amazing All-True Story of Juliette "Daisy" Gordon Low and Her Great Adventure*, Shana Corey
- *Katy and the Big Snow*, Virginia Lee Burton
- *Benjamin Franklin*, Wil Mara
- *Electric Ben: The Amazing Life and Times of Benjamin Franklin*, Robert Byrd
- *If You Lived in Colonial Times*, Ann McGovern
- *The House That George Built*, Suzanne Slade

## PLACES YOU CAN VISIT TO TALK ABOUT AMERICA, PAST AND PRESENT:

Visit a larger city or historic site together. Ask:

- What do you notice and wonder about the buildings and setting?
- How is life in this city different from or similar to our lives?
- Imagine visiting this place long ago. What might look different in the past? What has changed over time? What has stayed the same?

## CREDITS

Great Minds® has made every effort to obtain permission for the reprinting of all copyrighted material. If any owner of copyrighted material is not acknowledged herein, please contact Great Minds® for proper acknowledgment in all future editions and reprints of this module.

- All material from the *Common Core State Standards for English Language Arts & Literacy in History/Social Studies, Science, and Technical Subjects* © Copyright 2010 National Governors Association Center for Best Practices and Council of Chief State School Officers. All rights reserved.
- All images are used under license from Shutterstock.com unless otherwise noted.
- Lessons 2-5, pp. 45, 54, 68, 86: "The End" from NOW WE ARE SIX by A. A. Milne. Copyright 1927 by E. P. Dutton, renewed © 1955 by A. A. Milne. Used by permission of Dutton Children's Books, an imprint of Penguin Young Readers Group, a division of Penguin Random House LLC.
- For updated credit information, please visit http://witeng.link/credits.

## ACKNOWLEDGMENTS

### Great Minds® Staff

*The following writers, editors, reviewers, and support staff contributed to the development of this curriculum.*

Ann Brigham, Lauren Chapalee, Sara Clarke, Emily Climer, Lorraine Griffith, Emily Gula, Sarah Henchey, Trish Huerster, Stephanie Kane-Mainier, Lior Klirs, Liz Manolis, Andrea Minich, Lynne Munson, Marya Myers, Rachel Rooney, Aaron Schifrin, Danielle Shylit, Rachel Stack, Sarah Turnage, Michelle Warner, Amy Wierzbicki, Margaret Wilson, and Sarah Woodard.

### Colleagues and Contributors

*We are grateful for the many educators, writers, and subject-matter experts who made this program possible.*

David Abel, Robin Agurkis, Elizabeth Bailey, Julianne Barto, Amy Benjamin, Andrew Biemiller, Charlotte Boucher, Sheila Byrd-Carmichael, Eric Carey, Jessica Carloni, Janine Cody, Rebecca Cohen, Elaine Collins, Tequila Cornelious, Beverly Davis, Matt Davis, Thomas Easterling, Jeanette Edelstein, Kristy Ellis, Moira Clarkin Evans, Charles Fischer, Marty Gephart, Kath Gibbs, Natalie Goldstein, Christina Gonzalez, Mamie Goodson, Nora Graham, Lindsay Griffith, Brenna Haffner, Joanna Hawkins, Elizabeth Haydel, Steve Hettleman, Cara Hoppe, Ashley Hymel, Carol Jago, Jennifer Johnson, Mason Judy, Gail Kearns, Shelly Knupp, Sarah Kushner, Shannon Last, Suzanne Lauchaire, Diana Leddy, David Liben, Farren Liben, Jennifer Marin, Susannah Maynard, Cathy McGath, Emily McKean, Jane Miller, Rebecca Moore, Cathy Newton, Turi Nilsson, Julie Norris, Galemarie Ola, Michelle Palmieri, Meredith Phillips, Shilpa Raman, Tonya Romayne, Emmet Rosenfeld, Jennifer Ruppel, Mike Russoniello, Deborah Samley, Casey Schultz, Renee Simpson, Rebecca Sklepovich, Amelia Swabb, Kim Taylor, Vicki Taylor, Melissa Thomson, Lindsay Tomlinson, Melissa Vail, Keenan Walsh, Julia Wasson, Lynn Welch, Yvonne Guerrero Welch, Emily Whyte, Lynn Woods, and Rachel Zindler.

### Early Adopters

*The following early adopters provided invaluable insight and guidance for* Wit & Wisdom:

- Bourbonnais School District 53 • Bourbonnais, IL
- Coney Island Prep Middle School • Brooklyn, NY
- Gate City Charter School for the Arts • Merrimack, NH
- Hebrew Academy for Special Children • Brooklyn, NY
- Paris Independent Schools • Paris, KY
- Saydel Community School District • Saydel, IA
- Strive Collegiate Academy • Nashville, TN
- Valiente College Preparatory Charter School • South Gate, CA
- Voyageur Academy • Detroit, MI

Design Direction provided by Alton Creative, Inc.

Project management support, production design, and copyediting services provided by ScribeConcepts.com

Copyediting services provided by Fine Lines Editing

Product management support provided by Sandhill Consulting